What's in this book

This book belongs to

_____

眼镜在哪里？
Where are the glasses?

学习内容 Contents

沟通 Communication

说说家中的家具和物品
Talk about furniture and objects/items at home

生词 New words

★ 剪刀	scissors
★ 报纸	newspaper
★ 书架	bookcase
★ 沙发	sofa
★ 可能	may
★ 奇怪	strange
★ 又	again

茶几	coffee table
手表	watch
眼镜	glasses
觉得	to think
帮助	to help
衣柜	wardrobe

句式 Sentence patterns

您的眼镜又不见啦？

Are your glasses missing again?

文化 Cultures

中国传统家具

Traditional Chinese furniture

跨学科学习 Project

废物利用，制作收纳盒

Turn a shoe box into a storage box

Get ready

1 Have you ever lost something at home?

2 Do you keep your things organized?

3 Where did Hao Hao finally find his father's glasses?

qí guài
奇怪

"爸爸，您看，这些字真奇怪！三个
'木'，三个'口'……"浩浩说。

眼镜 (yǎn jìng)

沙发 (shā fā)

"我来看看。咦，我的眼镜呢？在沙发上吗？"爸爸说。

"您的眼镜又不见啦？茶几上只有剪刀和手表，没有眼镜。"浩浩说。

"我觉得它在报纸下面。"玲玲说。
"我觉得它在书架上面。"浩浩说。

"它可能在衣柜里吗？"浩浩问。
"眼镜在爸爸身上！"玲玲说。

"糟糕，中文书又不见了！"浩浩说。
"在这里。我们互相帮助。"爸爸说。

Let's think

1 Recall the story. Put a tick or a cross.

2 Let's tidy/clean up. Put the things where they belong and write the letters.

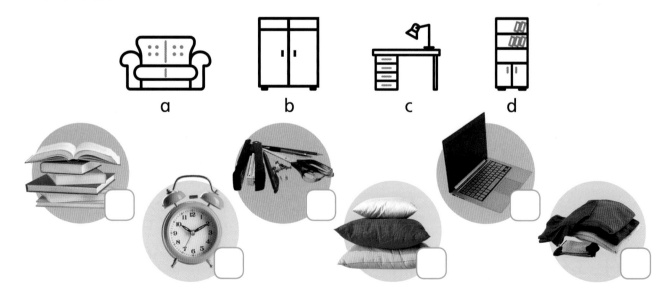

New words

 1 Learn the new words.

2 Listen to your teacher and point to the correct words above.

听听说说 Listen and say

 1 Listen and circle the mistakes.

 2 Look at the pictures. Listen to the story a

1

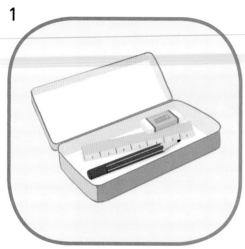

2

3

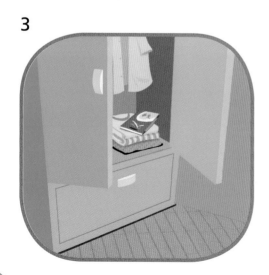

1

今天的报纸来了，爸爸在哪里呢？

他可能又在书房。

③

剪刀呢？剪刀在哪里？

剪刀在书架上，给你。

唉，这些是什么？真奇怪！

你觉得它们像什么呢？

小恐龙太可爱了！

我觉得你也很可爱！

a 帮助 b 衣柜 c 又
d 觉得 e 可能 f 手表

这是我的新 ___，
你 ___ 好看吗？

谢谢你！

不客气，我
们互相 ___。

我的帽子
___ 不见了。

它 ___ 在
___ 里面。

Task

Draw your living room or bedroom. Talk about it with your friend.

Game

Listen to your teacher and colour the furniture. Then match the correct words to them and write the letters.

a 书架　　b 沙发　　c 床　　d 茶几　　e 衣柜　　f 书桌

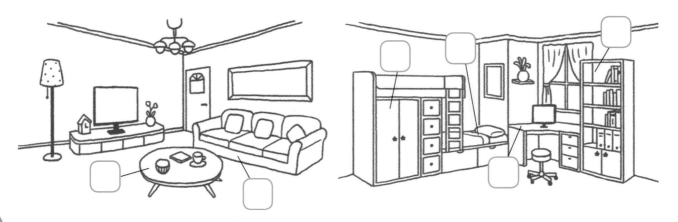

Chant

Listen and say.

眼镜在哪里呀？
眼镜不在报纸下，
也不在沙发上。
真奇怪呀真奇怪！

眼镜在哪里呀？
它可能在书架上，
也可能在衣柜里。
眼镜又跑去哪儿了？

生活用语 Daily expressions

真奇怪！
So strange!

我帮你。
Let me help you.

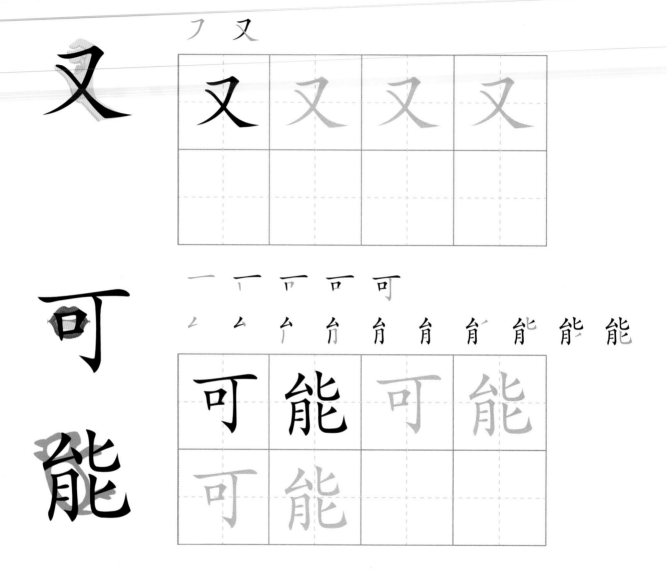

写一写 Write

1 Trace and write the characters.

ㄱ 又

又	又	又	又

一 ㄏ ㄇ 可 可

ㄥ ㄥ 夕 夕 夕 夕 夕 能 能

可	能	可	能
可	能		

2 Write and say.

这＿＿＿＿是爸爸的眼镜。

昨天　今天

今天中午，我＿＿吃了很多水果。

16

3 Fill in the blanks with the correct words. Colour the alarm clocks in the same colours.

又 　 学 　 衣服 　 想 　 早

今天＿＿上，我＿＿七点起床。洗脸、刷牙、穿＿＿＿＿，还找文具盒。

妈妈问："你＿＿做什么？"

我说："我去＿＿校。"

"今天是星期六，不用上＿＿。"妈妈说。

拼音输入法 Pinyin input

Type the missing words to complete the sentences. Number the sentences to make it a meaningful paragraph.

□ keai
但是我胖胖的，很＿＿＿。

□ mingzi
你好，我的＿＿＿叫熊猫。

□ hei　　bai
我的身体只有＿＿＿色和＿＿＿色。

□ dongwuyuan
快来＿＿＿找我吧！

17

Cultures

1 Traditional Chinese furniture has a long history and rich cultural style. What do you think?

Classical Chinese furniture is mostly made of wood, and built without any glue or nails.

衣柜

书架

书桌

椅子

沙发

茶几

2 Look at the pictures below and talk about them with your friend.

我觉得沙发很舒服。

我喜欢……

这个沙发很好看。

Project

1 Turn a shoe box into a storage box.

① ② ③ ④ ⑤ ⑥ ⑦

2 Tell your friend where the storage box is and what items it stores.

它在我的卧室……

它里面有玩具熊、羽毛球、手表……

温习 Checkpoint

1 Hao Hao and Brownie are in an unfamiliar room. Say the sentences to describe the room to them. Then write in the boxes.

5 这是什么画？它真奇怪！

4 书架上有书。

6 沙发真大，可以坐很多人。

3 报纸在桌子上。

7 茶几上有剪刀和手表。

2 我也觉得它很大。

8 树 ☐☐ 不是真的。

1 我觉得这个房间很大，也好很看。

2 Work with your friend. Colour the stars and the chillies.

Words	说	读	写
剪刀	☆	☆	🌶
报纸	☆	☆	🌶
书架	☆	☆	🌶
沙发	☆	☆	🌶
可能	☆	☆	☆
奇怪	☆	☆	🌶
又	☆	☆	☆
茶几	☆	🌶	🌶
手表	☆	🌶	🌶
眼镜	☆	🌶	🌶

Words and sentences	说	读	写
觉得	☆	🌶	🌶
帮助	☆	🌶	🌶
衣柜	☆	🌶	🌶
您的眼镜又不见啦？	☆	🌶	🌶

Talk about furniture and things at home	☆

3 What does your teacher say?

My teacher says ...

21

分享 Sharing

Words I remember

剪刀	jiǎn dāo	scissors
报纸	bào zhǐ	newspaper
书架	shū jià	bookcase
沙发	shā fā	sofa
可能	kě néng	may
奇怪	qí guài	strange
又	yòu	again
茶几	chá jī	coffee table
手表	shǒu biǎo	watch

眼镜	yǎn jìng	glasses
觉得	jué de	to think
帮助	bāng zhù	to help
衣柜	yī guì	wardrobe

Other words

咦	yí	(exclamation of surprise)
糟糕	zāo gāo	too bad
互相	hù xiāng	mutually

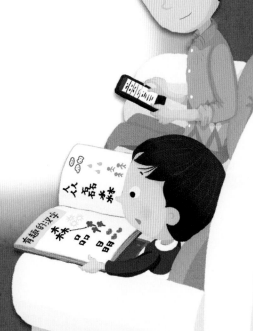

OXFORD
UNIVERSITY PRESS

Oxford University Press is a department of the University of Oxford.
It furthers the University's objective of excellence in research, scholarship,
and education by publishing worldwide. Oxford is a registered trade mark of
Oxford University Press in the UK and in certain other countries

Published in Hong Kong by
Oxford University Press (China) Limited
39th Floor, One Kowloon, 1 Wang Yuen Street, Kowloon Bay,
Hong Kong

Illustrated by Anne Lee, KK Ng, KY Chan and Wildman

Photographs for reproduction permitted by Dreamstime.com

China National Publications Import & Export (Group) Corporation is an authorized distributor of
Oxford Elementary Chinese.

Please contact content@cnpiec.com.cn or 86-10-65856782

ISBN: 978-0-19-047007-4

10 9 8 7 6 5 4 3 2